D1406243

Calvert County Public Library
P.O. Box 405
Prince Frederick, MD 20678

WEATHER WATCH

Frost
CAUSES AND EFFECTS

Philip Steele

Franklin Watts
New York London Toronto Sydney

© 1991 Franklin Watts

Franklin Watts
387 Park Avenue South
New York, NY 10016

Library of Congress Cataloging-in-Publication Data

Steele, Philip.
    Frost / Philip Steele.
        p. cm. -- (Weather watch)
    Includes index
    Summary: Discusses the climatic and meteorological conditions necessary
for frost to form and examines its effect on human, plant, and animal life.
        ISBN 0-531-11025-7
    1. Frost-- Juvenile literature. [1. Frost.] I. Title. II. Series: Steele, Philip.
Weather watch.
QC929. H6S74 1991
551.5'253--dc20   90-44596
                                                                        CIP
                                                                        AC

Printed in the United Kingdom

All rights reserved

Design: Jan Sterling
Picture researcher: Jennifer Johnson
Illustrator: Tony Kenyon, Gecko Ltd

Photograph acknowledgements

Cover (center) C R Varndell / Aquila Photographics, (outer) Geo Science
Features,
p1 Larry West / Frank Lane Picture Agency, p3 Roger Wilmshurst / Bruce
Coleman Ltd, p4 J Bastable / Frank Lane Picture Agency, p5 Larry West / Frank
Lane Picture Agency, p7 Roger Wilmshurst / Bruce Coleman Ltd, p8 Geo
Science Features, p9 Robin Scagell / Robert Harding Picture Agency, p10 Mary
Evans Picture Library, p12 Mark Newman / Frank Lane Picture Agency, p13
Novosti Press Agency, p14 M Nimmo / Frank Lane Picture Agency, p15 NASA /
Science Photo Library, p17 Martin Wandler / NHPA, p18 Winfried Wisniewski /
Frank Lane Picture Agency, p19 John Shaw / NHPA, p20 Doug Allan / Oxford
Scientific Films, p21 Hugh Clark / Frank Lane Picture Agency, p23 B & C
Alexander, p24 Steve McCutcheon / Frank Lane Picture Agency, p25 Mark
Wagner / Aviation Picture Library, p26 Ray Bird / Frank Lane Picture Agency,
p29 Trevor Hill.

Contents

Winter is coming

Skaters in Münster, Germany, wrap up warm. In frosty weather it is best to wear gloves and warm clothes. Frost can hurt the skin, causing chilblains or more severe damage. Children often give frost the nickname "Jack Frost," and say that he "nips" their fingers and toes.

In autumn, when the weather forecaster gives the first frost warning, it means winter is on its way. The earth becomes hard and cold and there is a chill in the air. Gardeners need to protect their plants.

Knowing when to expect frost is more important for gardeners and farmers than almost anyone else. This is because frost controls the length of the growing season. After the last spring frost, tender young plants can safely be left outside to produce flowers and fruit. The first frost of autumn kills many plants, and others stop flowering. Gardeners and farmers hope that the frost-free nights go on for as long as possible.

Water vapor tends to start condensing around specks of dust on cold surfaces. From these points, tiny ice crystals begin to spread outward. They build up needlelike structures, and stick together to form patterns.

The water cycle

Over two-thirds of our planet is covered in water. It runs from small streams into wide rivers and lakes, and empties into seas and oceans. Wherever the water is, it is part of a process called the **water cycle,** or hydrologic cycle. When the sun warms the surface of the earth, some of the water **evaporates**, or dries up. It forms an invisible gas called **water vapor** which is present in the air.

When the air cools, water vapor **condenses**, turning back into droplets of water. The droplets may form fog or mist, or collect as clouds and then fall as rain or snow. Some condenses at ground level, into droplets called **dew**.

Types of frost

The word frost is used to mean two different things. **Ground frost,** or white frost, is made up of frozen droplets of water. It covers the soil with a glistening, icy coat. In a severe frost, it covers windows, roofs and walls as well. This type of frost is also called **hoarfrost**.

The other kind of frost is **air frost**. Air frost occurs when the temperature in the air has dropped below 0°C (32°F), which is the **freezing point** of water.

How air frost forms

There are several ways in which the air can turn frosty. For example, when warm air rises, leaving the earth cool, winds from colder regions rush in to take its place.

Another cause of air frost is a combination of cold soil and sharp winds. Over the winter months, the soil gets colder and colder. A cold wind will quickly blow away any surface warmth, reducing the temperature still further. This effect is called **wind chill**.

How ground frost forms

When the leaves of plants or blades of grass become colder overnight than the air around them, the water vapor in the air condenses into dew. The temperature at which this happens is called the **dew point**, and it depends on how much moisture the air contains, or its **humidity**. A heavy dew soaks pavements and buildings as well as grass and plants. If the dewpoint is below 0°C (32°F), the water vapor turns into frozen droplets, or ground frost, instead of dew.

Frost, like snow, is made up of tiny **ice crystals**, and these are usually six-sided. Sometimes they are needle-shaped, or flat, or lie in layers that are long and rectangular (quartzlike). Occasionally, in the coldest weather, they are cube-shaped. The crystals form delicate, feathery and leafy patterns as they build up.

White hoarfrost on a cold winter's morning.

Ice formed on these shrubs when rain fell on the frozen branches.

Frosty conditions

Some frostlike conditions are not caused by freezing dew. **Rime** is formed when fog freezes on branches and twigs, giving them a thick, fuzzy, white coating. When rain freezes on contact with the ground or other objects whose surfaces are below freezing point, it forms a coating of solid ice.

Frost watch

On a day of heavy ground frost, check a section of grass in a park or garden. What area is covered in frost at, say, 7:00AM, 9:00AM, 11:00AM, 1:00PM and 3:00PM? Use a thermometer to record the temperature at each of these times of day.
How long does it take the sun to melt frost from the roofs? Can you see any plants that have suffered from frost damage?

Frosty weather

Dew and ground frost form overnight because that is when the temperature drops suddenly. If the temperature is above the freezing point, liquid droplets of dew are formed. At or below the freezing point, the water vapor turns into icy crystals of frost immediately, instead of becoming liquid first. Most frost forms on nights that are clear and windless. If there are low clouds, these act as a blanket, preventing warmth escaping from the surface of the land.

In winter, a clear, cold, starry night promises a heavy morning frost.

A Frost Fair on the frozen Thames in 1683.

✱ In most places, the frost melts when the sun's rays warm the air and the ground. However, one frost on the uplands of Dartmoor, in southern England, lasted for three months in the 1850s.

✱ Frost Fairs used to be held on the frozen River Thames in London, England. There were stalls and tents and fairground attractions. However, the Thames has not frozen over since the winter of 1813 to 1814. One reason for this is that the weather has become warmer. The city too has grown, with many heated buildings lining the banks. Another reason is that modern bridges allow the river to move faster, so that it is less likely to freeze over.

The pressure of air

The weight of air, or **atmosphere**, pressing down on the surface of the planet is called **air pressure**. Cold air presses down more heavily than warm air, creating areas of high pressure. Warm air expands and rises, creating areas of low pressure.

In areas of high pressure, there are few clouds in the sky because the water vapor in the air stays close to the ground. When the temperature falls, there is likely to be a frost. Areas of low pressure bring storms or rain clouds, and so are less likely to produce frosty weather.

Weather and climate

When the Southern Hemisphere tilts towards the sun, the season there changes to summer. At the same time, the Northern Hemisphere receives less light and heat, the temperature drops and winter brings frost and snow.

The weather in a particular place or country usually has a pattern over the years and this is known as its **climate**. Climate depends first of all on where a region is on the globe, and on whether it is beside the sea or in the middle of a continent. Winds and ocean currents also make a difference to the climate of a particular area.

The climate of an area is also affected by the angle of the earth as it travels around the sun. Parts of the planet warm up as they tilt towards the sun and become colder as they tilt away. This gives the changing seasons of summer and winter.

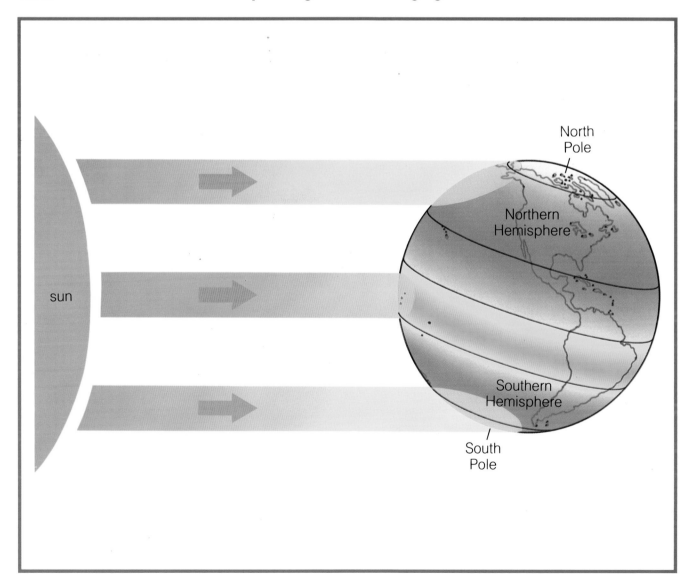

sun

North Pole

Northern Hemisphere

Southern Hemisphere

South Pole

At the Poles

Ice covers most of the Arctic Ocean while the land mass of Antarctica is covered by a permanent ice sheet more than 4,775 m (15,666 ft) thick in places. The climate at both Poles is harsh but a combination of cold air, high winds and blizzards makes Antarctica's climate the most severe in the world.

Icy plains called **tundra** surround the polar regions. The tundra is covered with snow for much of the year, although this melts during the brief summer in July and August. Then, flowers grow and animals nibble the mosses and lichens that can be seen for a short while. However, not far below the surface, the soil of the tundra remains frozen all year around. This is called **permafrost**, and it is like a vast freezer. The frozen remains of mammoths, the giant elephants of prehistory, have been found buried in the permafrost. They had lain underground for tens of thousands of years, so perfectly preserved by the cold that their flesh was still fresh enough to be eaten.

The surface of the tundra melts for about four months each year. Pools of water gather on the surface and plants flower, attracting insects. Caribou feed off mosses and lichens. Heavy frosts, followed by ice and snow, soon return. The deeper layers of soil remain frozen all the time.

A baby mammoth, 10,000 years old, being lifted from the Siberian permafrost.

✳ Permafrost has been found to a depth of over 1,370 m (4,495 ft) in the Siberia region of the Soviet Union.

✳ The coldest town in the world is also in the eastern Soviet Union. Oymyakon has experienced temperatures of -68°C (-90°F).

A frost-free future?

Over many millions of years, the world's climate has changed. There have been bitterly cold periods, known as **ice ages**, and warmer periods, known an **interglacials**. Scientists now believe that the world is warming up - and very rapidly. This **global warming** is partly the result of people burning fuels and gases.

The tropics

Ground frost is rare in the warmth of the tropics, although frost does sometimes form in deserts like the Sahara. There are few clouds over deserts, and so the nights are clear but cold. Dew and frost are often the only source of moisture in desert regions.

Temperate regions

Between the icy polar regions and the tropics are regions with a mild, or **temperate**, climate. Temperate regions far from the sea have cold, frosty winters and dry, hot summers. This is because there is less moisture in the air than in countries beside the sea. Coastal regions have wetter, warmer climates with less frost, because moisture from the ocean creates clouds that keep the land warmer.

Temperate regions have four seasons: spring, summer, autumn and winter. Ground frost is common in autumn, winter and spring, but rare in summer.

Weather signs

Farmers and gardeners keep a close eye on the weather because of the damage that frost can cause. They check the temperature of the air and the ground, and look at how much cloud there is. They also check the direction of the wind. Crisp, cold weather, a clear sky, or high icy clouds, all give warning of frosty weather.

A late spring frost turned these fir trees brown. People sometimes talk of plants being "scorched" by frost, because they shrivel up as if they had been burned.

Frost damages some crops and kills others. Root crops, like carrots, can become blackened and die. A late spring frost can destroy the buds and also the blossoms of fruit trees, which means a loss of income for fruit farmers. Citrus fruit crops, like oranges and lemons, are often at risk, especially when the fruit is forming.

Forecasts and records

✳ The amount of water vapor in the air, the humidity, is measured with a wet-bulb thermometer. This is a thermometer with its bulb covered with a wet cloth. As the water evaporates from the cloth, the mercury in the thermometer drops. Its reading is subtracted from the temperature recorded by an ordinary thermometer. The difference between the two, when worked out against a scale, gives the percentage of moisture in the air.

✳ The distance from sea level to the base of a cloud is measured in meters. The amount of cloud covering the sky is measured in **oktas**, or eighths. A **cloud cover** of eight oktas stretches across the whole of the sky, and a cloud cover of one okta covers only one-eighth of the sky.

Scientific instruments are used to forecast weather conditions. Temperature is measured with thermometers, and **barometers** are used to check the pressure of the atmosphere. If the air pressure is high and the temperature low, frost is more likely.

The scientific study of the weather is called **meteorology**. Meteorologists work at **weather stations** all over the world, gathering information from many different sources. Instruments in balloons and planes record conditions in the atmosphere. Weather satellites out in space, such as Meteosat, send back pictures of the cloud patterns around the earth, as well as wind force and direction, and temperature changes.

This picture was taken by a weather satellite. It shows the cloud cover over the Florida peninsula.

A maximum-minimum thermometer. Alcohol expands 10 times more than mercury. When it is warm, the alcohol pushes the mercury around the tube into a vacuum.

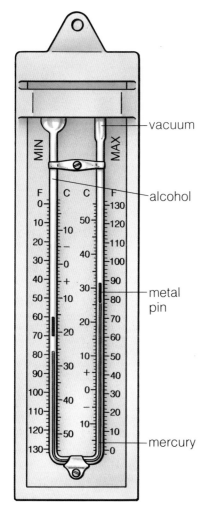

Weather forecasts on television and radio can now tell us with greater accuracy what weather conditions we can expect for several days ahead. Forecasters now use computers to speed up their study of weather conditions.

Average temperatures

Meteorologists need to work out average temperatures. To do this, they use a maximum-minimum thermometer which records the highest and lowest temperatures during the day. A maximum-minimum thermometer has a U-shaped tube containing alcohol and mercury. As the temperature rises, the alcohol expands, pushing the mercury up the right hand column into a vacuum. Resting on top of the mercury is a metal pin. As the temperature falls, the alcohol contracts, and the mercury slides down the right hand arm and rises up the left hand arm. The metal pin is left behind, marking the highest temperature reached. A second metal pin resting on the left-hand column of mercury records the lowest temperature. Each day, a magnet is used to pull the pins down so that they rest once more on the columns of mercury.

Keep a temperature record

If you have a maximum-minimum thermometer at your school, record the highest and lowest temperatures each day in your weather notebook. Add together each pair of figures and divide by two to find the average daily temperature. Then add these figures together and divide by seven to find the average weekly temperature.

Frost and landscape

Snow and frost fill the cracks and crevices at Bryce Canyon, in Utah. Millions of years ago these rocks were formed from the sludge at the bottom of ancient seas and rivers. They were pressed by the forces of the earth until they became hard. Then they were worn down by wind and rain, and frozen by winter frosts. Frost eats away at the rock faces, cracking and crumbling them.

As water in the soil freezes, it takes up more space, breaking down the thick clods of earth into fine, crumbly soil. This makes it easier for new plants to take root when the spring arrives.

Frost also attacks stones and slabs of rock. Year after year, rocks are heated by the sun, and this makes them expand, or stretch. Then they are frozen by frost, and this causes them to contract, or shrink. Over time, this treatment makes rocks begin to crack and crumble. As small pieces fall, the wind lashes them against the rock face, and so they are broken down still further into grit and sand. This whole process is called **weathering**.

The grit and sand are washed away by rivers. In places, the water leaves behind some of the grit and sand, and sometimes it begins to build up into new rocks.

Frost and the natural world

Gardeners and farmers have to protect plants and food crops against frost. Crops can be covered with a loose **mulch** of straw, leaves or peat, or with sacking or plastic sheeting. Some plants are grown in greenhouses to keep them warm and frost-free.

Seedlings need special care, and small glass or polyethylene-covered frames, called cold-frames, are placed over them to keep out the frost.

Greenhouses allow flowers to be grown even in places with a fairly harsh climate, such as Iceland. This greenhouse is heated by hot, natural springs on the hillside.

To prevent a ground frost forming in the first place, smoky fires are lit and sometimes fields are flooded. In the orange groves of California, for instance, gas burners are used to keep frost at bay. These methods keep the air temperature just above freezing, so that the plants are not damaged.

Although many plants are damaged by frost, others have **adapted** to cold climates. Conifers, such as fir and pine trees, protect their seeds inside scaly cones, and have needles instead of broad leaves. Frosty uplands are the home of low-growing tough shrubs such as juniper and bilberry.

The alpine bearberry grows on the lower slopes of Mount McKinley in Alaska, the highest peak in North America. Shrubs have to be tough to survive frosty winters in the mountains.

Some small flowering plants known as **alpines** can survive on bitterly cold mountain slopes. One of the best known of these is the edelweiss, which has small white flowers in the summer. The leaves and flowers are furry, and this helps them to resist the hardest frost as they cling to the ground in rocky crevices. The purple saxifrage is another hardy plant. It can live on soil that is regularly broken up by severe frosts. Its evergreen leaves trail over the cold ground, forming a dense mat.

Animal survival

Frosty weather causes problems for many animals. Water freezes over and food becomes scarce. It is difficult for birds to find enough food to keep them alive and many die from the cold.

Animals have found various ways to survive the frost. At the first sign of cold weather, many **migrate**, traveling long distances each autumn to places with warmer climates where there is also a supply of food.

◄ An adult emperor penguin protects its three-week old chick from the chilling Antarctic winds.

► Some animals, like this dormouse, hibernate during the winter. During this period their body weight is halved, and their heartbeat almost stops. Their body temperature drops, but it must never fall below freezing, or the animals would die. Here the dormouse's body is protected from the frost by a snug nest built in the hedges.

✽ During the Arctic summer, hundreds of different kinds of birds feed on the tundra, but few stay to face the freezing winter. One that does is the snowy owl, which feeds on small rodents called lemmings.

✽ The emperor penguin's egg needs a temperature of above 33°C (91°F) to hatch out. However, in Antarctica where it lives, there may be 50 degrees of frost. So the male penguin rests the egg on his feet and folds his belly around it. He keeps the egg warm like this for eight weeks until it hatches.

Other animals **hibernate**. As the temperature drops, they bury themselves in the ground, or hide away in caves or hollow trees. Their body temperature falls, and their heart rate and breathing slow down. They use less energy in this state and therefore need less food. Dormice eat much more than usual in the early autumn. Then they go into a deep sleep until the spring, living on the fat stored in their bodies.

Black bears become drowsy. They doze in their dens most of the winter, coming out only on warmer days to search for food. Food helps to keep the body warm, and a number of animals store up food at the beginning of winter. Squirrels hide away piles of nuts. Beavers cut up twigs to eat and store them underwater before the lakes freeze over. Snails hide away in cracks in walls. To prevent their moist bodies from freezing, some snails can seal up the opening of their shells.

Many mammals grow a thicker coat of fur or hair during the winter. In the spring they **molt**, losing the extra hair as the weather becomes warmer. Birds keep out the cold by fluffing out their feathers to create a warm layer of air around their bodies.

Helping the birds

In frosty weather, when the earth becomes hard and icy, birds need an extra supply of food to give them energy and warmth.

Make a simple bird table and attach it either to a branch or to an upright pole. An upside-down plastic bowl or cookie tin attached to the upright pole will prevent cats from climbing onto the table. Put out scraps of cheese, bacon rind or crusts of brown bread.

Chickadees will enjoy peanuts from a mesh bag, or a "pudding" made of melted fat, cereal and scraps.

Grow trees and garden shrubs like cotoneaster, holly or rowan, which have berries on them in the autumn.

Put out a water bowl for the birds, and don't forget to remove the ice from the surface when it freezes.

Put your bird table where you can see it from a nearby window, and watch the birds feeding. Use a bird book to help you to identify the different types of birds and record which birds feed at your table. Keep a record of which birds you see mostly in winter, and which birds you see in summer only. Do any birds visit the table all year around?

Frost and humans

When people breathe out in frosty air, their breath can be seen. This is because the water vapor in it condenses to form water droplets as the warm breath meets the cold air.

Humans react to frosty air in other ways. In cold weather, the skin forms little bumps, sometimes called goose bumps. They are caused by the muscles that raise small hairs on the body. In the same way that birds fluff out their feathers, people raise these hairs to create a layer of warm air around their bodies. Another human protection against cold is shivering. Tiny jerks by the muscles under the skin make the muscles work harder. This helps make extra heat to warm the body up.

Mountain climbers at a camp in Kashmir. During their climb they may need to bivouac, or sleep out, in the open. Special clothes and materials help them to survive heavy frosts.

One of the things that keep humans warm is blood, which is carried in a maze of tiny tubes called blood vessels. When the weather is very cold, the blood vessels near the skin stop working. This stops heat escaping through the skin. It makes people look pale and even slightly blue.

To avoid frostbite, people who work in polar regions have to be sure to keep their ears, nose, feet and hands covered.

Danger from frost

One of the greatest dangers in really cold weather is **hypothermia**. It is caused by the body temperature dropping too low. The first signs are clumsiness, shivering and a pale skin. Gentle warming is necessary, otherwise the person will become unconscious and die. Those people most likely to suffer from hypothermia are the aged, babies, and stranded mountaineers or shipwrecked sailors.

Sometimes, the skin and flesh actually freeze. When this happens, there is a prickly feeling in the toes, fingers, nose or ears, and the flesh turns black and blue, or white. The skin becomes hard and loses all feeling. The damage caused is called **frostbite**. Explorers in the Arctic or Antarctic can suffer from frostbite that goes as deep as the bone. If they are not rescued by plane and rushed to the hospital, they might lose the part of the body that has been frostbitten.

Frost damage

Frost affects towns and transportation in many ways. Buses, trains and planes may all be delayed because of frost and freezing fog. Surfaces become slippery and dangerous for walking and driving. People fall and hurt themselves, and cars skid.

To help to prevent accidents, the roads are sprinkled with cinders, sand or salt. Switches on railway lines are heated so that they do not ice up. Car radiators could burst if the water in them froze and expanded, and so a mixture of chemicals called antifreeze is used to lower the freezing point of the water. It has to be poured in before the first sign of frosty weather.

In frosty weather, planes are sprayed with de-icer before they take off. Any ice that forms, especially on the wings, will affect the plane's handling as it tries to gain height. Several planes have crashed due to ice on their wings.

Water gushing out of a burst pipe has formed an ice sheet over the side of this farm building and farm yard.

Building and engineering

Frost can damage houses and other buildings. Tiles or bricks that soak up moisture often crack open and crumble after frosty weather. If water pipes freeze, they burst as the water expands into ice. Then when the ice in the pipes melts, water floods into the house. Pipes and water tanks need to be protected by padding, called **lagging**.

Buildings lose heat if they are not properly **insulated**. Insulation around doors prevents heat escaping as well as stopping cold drafts from entering. Attic spaces are usually padded with fiberglass or other material to stop heat escaping through the roof. Windows fitted with double-glazing, made from two sheets of glass with a space between, keep the cold out and the heat in.

Engineers have to allow for very cold temperatures when they build bridges. Many bridges are made of steel which expands when the weather is hot and contracts when it is cold. To make a bridge safe, expansion joints are built into it to allow for this. The joints allow the metal to move very slightly as it expands or contracts.

Shrink and stretch

Test how metal expands and contracts at different temperatures.

Find an empty plastic bottle with a screw-on cap. Put on the lid.

Run warm water on the plastic sides and cold water on the cap. How easy is it to unscrew?

Next, run warm water on the cap and cold water on the plastic. Does it open more easily? Why?

Making frost

Frost does have it uses for humans. Thousands of years ago, people found that if they left food buried in the snow, it would stay fresh. Food goes bad because **bacteria** grow on it. They spread most quickly when the food is warm, so a freezing temperature makes it keep better.

For many years people built ice boxes and cool cellars for storing their food. Then in 1834 Jacob Perkins, an American living in England, found that by making fluids evaporate and then condense over and over again, he could cool surfaces and make artificial frost.

The idea was taken up by other inventors, and by 1861 the first refrigerators were on sale. Another 62 years later, in 1923, the first electric refrigerators were built in Sweden.

In a refrigerator, liquid is pumped through a series of tubes. As it turns into vapor, it absorbs heat from the refrigerator and makes it very cold. When the vapor turns back to liquid, it gives off the heat it has absorbed into the room.

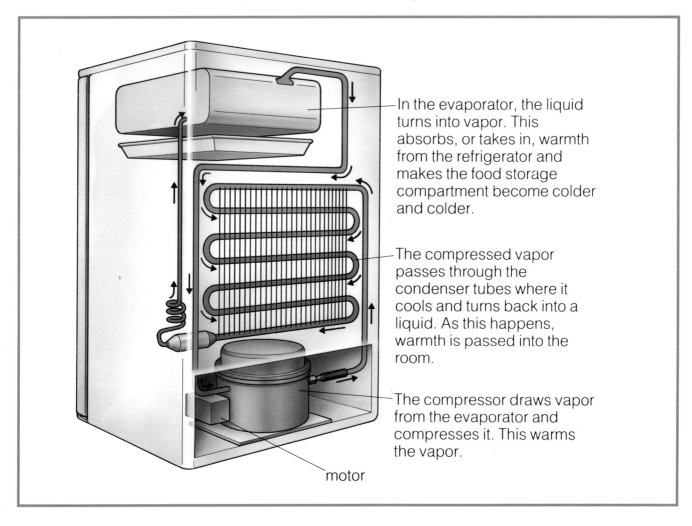

In the evaporator, the liquid turns into vapor. This absorbs, or takes in, warmth from the refrigerator and makes the food storage compartment become colder and colder.

The compressed vapor passes through the condenser tubes where it cools and turns back into a liquid. As this happens, warmth is passed into the room.

The compressor draws vapor from the evaporator and compresses it. This warms the vapor.

motor

The inside of a freezer is coated with machine-made frost. Low temperatures keep food fresh.

Freezing food

In 1924, an American firm started to produce ready-frozen foods which could be stored for a long period. Fresh foods have to be frozen very quickly at temperatures of -25°C to -34°C (-13°F to -29°F) in order to keep their shape and flavor. Then they have to be stored at -18°C (-0.4°F).

The big freeze

Prepare trays of ice cubes in the freezer compartment of a refrigerator. Remove the trays and try this experiment.

How long can you keep an ice cube from melting? You must not put it back in the refrigerator, but you can use any kitchen materials that you think might keep it cool.

How quickly can you melt an ice cube without using artificial heat?

Glossary

adapt   To alter or change to suit a different purpose or different surroundings.

air frost   The condition of the air when it falls below a temperature of 0°C (32°F).

air pressure   The force with which air presses down on the surface of the planet.

alpine   Belonging to a mountain region. Alpine flowering plants are small and tough.

atmosphere   The layer of gases and dust that forms the air around a planet.

bacteria   Tiny creatures that can be seen only with a strong microscope.

barometer   An instrument for measuring air pressure.

climate   The typical weather pattern in a region.

cloud cover   The amount of the sky covered by clouds.

condense   To become more dense. When vapor condenses it turns into liquid.

dew   Moisture that forms on the ground or other objects overnight.

dew point   The temperature at which the vapor in the air turns into dew.

evaporate   To turn into vapor.

freezing point   The temperature at which a liquid or gas freezes. The freezing point of water is 0°C (32°F).

frostbite   Damage to human skin and flesh caused by very low temperatures.

global warming   The rapid warming of the earth's climate, possibly as a result of air pollution.

ground frost   A coating of ice crystals on cold ground or other objects, formed overnight from the moisture in the air.

hibernate   To sleep deeply through the winter. Many animals hibernate for long periods in order to stay alive.

hoarfrost   A thick, white ground frost.

humidity   The amount of moisture in the air.

hypothermia An unusually low body temperature.

ice age A period in the earth's history when snow and ice spread far into the temperate regions.

ice crystals Patterned structures which grow as water vapor freezes.

insulate To prevent the escape of heat.

interglacial A period between ice ages, when the earth's climate becomes warmer.

lagging Padding wound around pipes and water tanks to stop water freezing.

meteorology The scientific study of weather conditions in the air which surrounds our planet.

migrate To travel a long distance to find better conditions. Many birds and animals migrate in order to avoid icy winter weather or to search for food.

molt To lose hair, fur or feathers.

mulch A covering of material used to protect plants.

okta A unit for measuring cloud cover.

permafrost A layer of soil which remains frozen all the time because of the polar climate.

rime A thick coating of frosty ice formed by freezing fog.

temperate Having a mild climate, like the lands between the tropics and the polar regions.

tundra The vast plains of the far north. Deep down, the soil of the tundra remains frozen all year around. The snows melt during the summer months, allowing some plants to flower.

water cycle (hydrologic cycle) The endless process by which rain falls, turns into vapor, rises, turns into droplets, and falls back to earth.

water vapor An invisible gas in the air. Water becomes vapor when it dries out or evaporates.

weather station A base for the scientific recording of weather conditions.

weathering The effect of the weather on the landscape and on buildings.

wind chill The cooling effect of wind at low temperatures.

Index

Calvert County Public Library
P.O. Box 405
Prince Frederick, MD 20678